The Constructor

ALSO BY JOHN KOETHE

Poetry
   Blue Vents
   Domes
   The Late Wisconsin Spring
   Falling Water

Philosophy
   The Continuity of Wittgenstein's Thought

Essays
   Poetry at One Remove

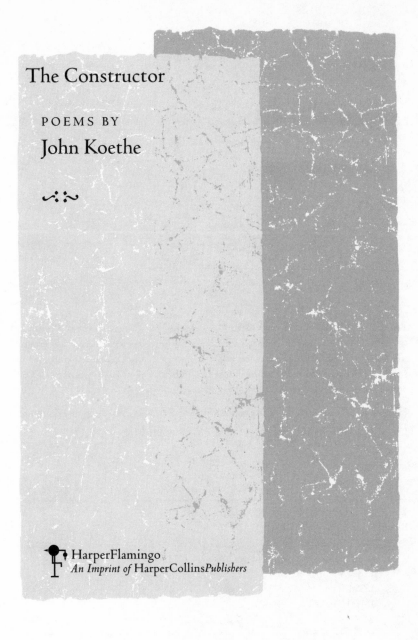

The Constructor

POEMS BY

John Koethe

HarperFlamingo
An Imprint of HarperCollinsPublishers

HarperCollins books may be purchased for educational, business, or sales promotional use. For information please write: Special Markets Department, HarperCollins Publishers, Inc., 10 East 53rd Street, New York, NY 10022.

FIRST EDITION
Designed by Jeanette Olender

Library of Congress Cataloging-in-Publication Data
Koethe, John, 1945–
 The constructor : poems / John Koethe. —1st ed.
  p. cm.
  ISBN 0-06-019303-4
  I. Title.
  PS3561.035C66 1999
  811'.54—dc21   98-30755 CIP

99 00 01 02 03 ❖/HC 10 9 8 7 6 5 4 3 2 1

In memoriam
Willy Eisenhart and Geoffrey Joseph

Acknowledgments

I am grateful to the editors of *The Paris Review* for awarding the 1986 Bernard F. Conners Award to "Mistral"; to the editors of *Southwest Review* for awarding the 1989 Elizabeth Machette Stover Award to "The Waiting Game"; and to the John Simon Guggenheim Memorial Foundation, the Milwaukee Arts Foundation, and the National Endowment for the Arts for fellowships that were of great help in writing many of these poems.

Contents

Sunday Evening   1

The Saturday Matinee   3

Pining Away   5

"I Heard a Fly Buzz . . ."   7

The Other Condition   9

Mistral   13

The Waiting Game   24

Between the Lines   26

Threnody for Two Voices   29

Un Autre Monde   33

A Perspective Box   34

The Advent of the Ordinary   37

What the Stars Meant   39

The Constructor   43

Fleeting Forms of Life   50

Au Train   52

The Lake of White Flowers   55

A Parking Lot with Trees   56

Permissions Acknowledgments   61

About the Author   63

The Constructor

Sunday Evening

Ideas as crystals and the logic of a violin:
The intricate evasions warming up again
For another raid on the inarticulate. And soon
The morning melody begins, the oranges and the tea,
The introspective walk about the neighborhood,
The ambient noise, the low lapping of water over stones.
The peace one finds encounters one alone,
In the memories of books, or half-remembered songs,
Or in the mild enchantments of the passive mood:
To hesitate, to brood, to linger in the library and then,
As from some green and sunny chair, arise and go.
The noons seem darker, and the adolescent
Boys who used to hang around the parking lot are gone.
More water in the eyes, more dissonant musicians in the subways,
And from the font of sense a constant, incidental drone.
It *is* a kind of reconfiguration, and the solitary exercise
That seeks to reaffirm its name seems hollow. The sun is lower in
  the sky,
And as one turns towards what had felt like home,
The windows start to flicker with a loveless flame,
As though the chambers they concealed were empty. Is this
How heaven feels? The same perspective from a different room,
Inhabiting a prospect seen from someone else's balcony
In a suspended moment—as a silver airplane silently ascends
And life, at least as one has known it, slides away?

I thought that people understood these things.
They show the gradual encroachment of a vast,

Impersonal system of exchanges on that innermost domain
In which each object meant another one, all singing each to each
In a beautiful regress of forgetting. Nature as a language
Faithful to its terms, yet with an almost human face
That took the dark, romantic movements of desire, love, and loss
And gave them flesh and brought them into view;
Replaced by emblems of a rarefied sublime,
Like Cantor's Paradise, or Edward Witten staring into space
As the leaves fell and a little dog raced through them in the park.
Was any of that mine? Was it ever anyone's?
Time makes things seem more solid than they were,
Yet these imaginary things—the dolphins and the bells, the sunny
    terrace
And the bright, green wings, the distant islet on the lake—
Were never barriers, but conditions of mere being, an enchanting haze
That takes one in and like a mild surprise gives way,
As though the things that one had strained against were shards of
    space.
The evening air feels sweeter. The moon,
Emerging from a maze of clouds into the open sky,
Casts a thin light on the trees. Infinitely far away,
One almost seems to hear—as though the fingers of a solitary giant
Traced the pure and abstract schema of those strings
In a private movement of delight—the soundless syllables'
Ambiguous undulations, like the murmur of bees.

The Saturday Matinee

Forgotten strings. A woman wearing black leans back against a
    mantelpiece.
The view from where *I* sat was of a street above a canyon,
And the story was a melodrama with a cast of four.
The subject was an ordinary way of life, defined by principles
I'd usually ignore, and messages that came to me in

Words that I'd eventually forget, or hadn't actually understood.
Yet now and then I'd have a dream in which a feeble light was visible
    beneath my door,
And unfamiliar voices mumbled in the kitchen; and then I'd wake up
    in a sweat
And feel the language closing in like traces of the people who'd been
Close to me at different stages of my childhood,

Mouthing a kind of rhetoric I thought I'd long ago outgrown,
Whose undisguised appeal could reach me like a popular song,
Directly and without any hesitation; or like a movie,
Strong and sentimental, filled with images of faces I could feel.
—Cut to home: the summer slides away in pages,

And the dreams that used to trouble me occur less frequently.
Sometimes I sit here, waiting in my mind as in the
Theaters where I'd watched them gravitate across the screen,
Vacant beneath the skin, projecting the emotions they were made
    to feel
And breathing in the atmosphere of infantile

Rage that lets them remain alive. And I can hear them
In the lyrics of a song accompanying a private tune, the argument
    concealed in a lament
—Although I realize no argument can bring them back to me,
Or let me speak to them again. I sit here mulling over moments
With the flesh scooped out, the impulse spent

And feeling nothing but the words—like Scarlett, in a furnished
    room,
Imagining her abandoned house, immense and uninhabited
And filled with silence and the sound of birds, its rafters open to the
    weather,
Dust motes floating through the air that X and Y had breathed
—Only no one misses them, and no one cares.

Where do words go, once the hurt that puffed them up has healed?
The private ones still hurt. But publicly, a sort of calm prevails,
As a door bangs, or a car drives past the corner, or overhead a cloud
    goes sailing by
And gradually their stories disappear like wonderful balloons
Rising straight into the sky, on an August day.

Pining Away

It was suspiciously easy, with no place to hide and,
At the same time, no one to hide from. No one wondered
Where anything went, for it seemed impossible to imagine
A greater form of happiness, content just to let things go
But wondering nevertheless, in those first expansive
Speculations of self-consciousness, what the face meant,
And whether anything other than its own companionable
Intelligence might be discovered there. The answer came
Evasively, and with averted eyes, as the half-remembered
Promises that time had murmured to disguise its emptiness
Began to seem like vestiges of something still indubitably
Real, which time and memory would instinctively recover
Sooner or later, as the minutes slid relentlessly away
And the memories sank into unconsciousness, like myths.

So this is how the genius of reflection came to feel,
Imprisoned in its self-consuming enterprise that still
Continues to reverberate throughout the universe, now
Of the contracting kind, and incapable of withstanding
The hole in its own imagination. But it stays there
In a small, damp room, where a style of diffidence
Allows it to negotiate each day without the fear
Of being deflected from its predetermined course
Around the deserted library, steadily getting nearer,
Asymptotically approaching its interior destination
Until suddenly arrested on the verge of misunderstanding

By those syllables erupting like quick flashes from a mind
Like a sputtering lamp, throwing the collapsing shadows
Into stark relief, while Echo hesitates as the brief
Disruption fades, the scattering rays are gathered
In the nick of time, and the hourglass is inverted.

"I Heard a Fly Buzz . . ."

for Bruce and Livija Renner

Light began to wane; it was supernaturally calm.
There was movement in the air, yet nothing moving when I looked.
I felt an inkling of the night that never came, the
Faint pre-echo of a noise I couldn't hear, or didn't want to hear—
Either from timidity, or fear, or an exaggerated sense of duty;
Or because I'd spent a lifetime trying to be good.
I thought I heard a tune from a calliope, and pieces of a
Prayer I used to say each night before I went to bed—
Now I lay me down to sleep—while a parade of images of
Neighborhoods I'd known, and friends whose humor I'd enjoyed
Meandered through my consciousness like numbers in a
Stark, mechanical affair of abstract objects in a void
—For they'd begun to feel as distant as an evening
In Balboa Park, with most of them dying, and some already dead,
Inhabiting a long, generic memory only I could read.
Life ends on a particular day, and at a particular time; and yet I
    thought that
I inhabited a world existing entirely in my head, in a constructed space
Where it was never any special time, or hot, or on a Tuesday
When the phone rang, or with the television on. I
Think that I was wrong to see my body as a kind of place
From which the soul, as entropy increases, migrates
In an upward-moving spiral of completion, a defining state
—But a subtractive one—that brings relief from hope
And freedom from complexity, escaping one by one the

Emblems of its former life and then, the waiting over,
The repentance done, ascending in a final sacrament of light into a
Vacuum filled with comprehending angels who might sing to me.
    Instead,
I found myself back home in California, sipping coffee
While an unknown insect flew, invisible, around my head.
The texture of a certain summer day came back to me,
But now in a heightened form, the simple sweetness of its presence
Mingled with the faint, metallic taste of fear, until
Each moment meant two things. The nearer I approached,
The more inscrutable it seemed. The tiny buzzing noise became an
    avalanche of
Sound whose overriding meaning was the same: *get out of here*
—Wherever "here" might be. And something spoke to me,
But when I turned around and looked I caught the image of my own
    complacency
Reflected in a mirror—a temperament defined by childish anecdotes
    and jokes
And focused on an object of dispassionate concern
Beyond itself, yet part of my experience. I finally came to see
That what I valued was a fragile and contingent life
Supported by the thought of something *opposite* that might,
At any time, break through its thin veneer. Yet all the time,
Despite that constant sense, it felt so sure, so solid.
I remember walking through a park . . .
                                    And suddenly
My world felt light, then numb, and then abruptly clear.
Some faces suddenly ballooned, then blurred.
Then it got dark.

The Other Condition

The utopia of the Other Condition gets displaced by the empirical attitude. . . . The utopia of the pure Other Condition empties or branches into God.
ROBERT MUSIL

It eases care. And I wanted something,
But the form of my conception was so bare and
Featureless that almost nothing tangible
Could fulfill that need. It was not enough,
Though the inspiration lingered, cold and barely
Conscious of itself amid the private, pastel
Shadings and pervasive warmth, but utterly alone.
I wanted to conceive the solid song that lasts
Beyond mere memory, the vast sky entering a mind and
Gleaming there, like someone's past emerging from a
Long, involuntary dream into the unforgiving light of
Other people's feelings and the weight of the external
Obstacles that greet it, which it can't identify.
For I thought I was a stranger too, and that my real
Happiness lay somewhere in that past, beyond mere care
And reason, in the memory—or in the fantasy—of home.
How suddenly the recognitions came, and the insane
Anger that defined each moment that glared back at me,
But which has finally come to characterize my life.
What is it to be alive? And they linger in the night
Like dream words arguing their dark, unsuitable desires

That render it complete, both the concrete experiences
Sheltered in the heart, as well as those imaginary
Parts it can't possess, from that first sweet breath
Of summer to the thin, attenuated voice descanting in
An amber light, as if sheer consciousness could reach
All the way to its horizon, which is death.

It's all ambience, without any density or shape,
An intense atmosphere of grace and disappointment
With the unclarity of real life and the dead certainty
Of abstraction, like a sense of something intimate and
Strange beyond the reach of feeling. Yet out of it
The strain of day-to-day existence flows, the vagrant
Moods and platitudes that come to seem the outward form
Of one's essential being, like a gradually remembered
Melody emerging from a cave. I'd never really known
How intricate a tone of voice could be, or how evasive
The direct approach to life could finally become.
A minor shading or the faint intoxication of a word
Held in the mind—is that all sensibility can see
In its pristine innocence, and all the insubstantial,
Floating intellect that seeks to understand itself
Can understand? Nothing can bring its fragrance back
Or make it breathe again, and the traces that accumulate
As time fades mimic the appearance of unconsciousness,
Portraying it, like some primitive fabulist of the self,
Immediately, but with a miserable detachment and the
Kind of understanding that only emerges later on,
And in somebody else, and in a different form.

◆ ◆

I have this life, and still remain dissatisfied.
Objects change, yet keep their separate trajectories,
And nothing stays. I wander through a day as someone
Else might wander quietly through my mind, and the numb
Tranquillity that covers me each night seems meaningless.
Out in the world my themes deteriorate and die.
What if these thoughts were just recalcitrant desires
Felt as despair, and all these computations of the mind
Merely sensations? The abstract darkness, death, would
Still be there and unimaginable, shadowing the years
Life wasted while the atmosphere of waiting dissipated
And the body came to realize itself, and to feel afraid.
How should one live? I kept the primitive fear at bay
By hiding it behind a screen of intimate description,
A protective diary, or concealing it inside of a serene,
Expedient creation whose insides were empty and whose
Shell was just an accidental mass of scraps and stitches,
Yet which to me has come to feel seamless and complete.
Year after year the elemental dreams keep reoccurring—
That if I could find my way to set tomorrow free again,
Or to return to sheer existence . . . Incrementally,
Like an approaching equinox, the alternating styles
Of passionate, subdued reflection, and then difference
And stillness seem to chasten and revise each other,
Until finally they realize a kind of rough equivalence.
And it seems enough. It represents a form of life
Like this one, one confined to ordinary happiness
With nothing else—nothing unasked for, unimaginable

Or unmeant—beyond its facts of consciousness and
Tense and that peculiar sense of peace that comes
As one gets older, with the waning of the fundamental
Fear of something that might be merely one's self—
As though the ache were empty and this life
Completely adequate, with rationalizing memories
And afterthoughts to render it precisely
Equal to its task, and yet not enough.

Mistral

I.

There seems to be, about certain lives,
A vague, violent frame, an imperceptible
Halo of uncertainty, diffidence, and taste
Worn like a private name that only God knows,
Echoing what it hides, that floats above a bottomless
Anxiety that underlies their aura of remote calm.
The intense half-dreams accumulate behind a smile;
The mind hesitates in its reflection, but remains alone.
Part of their story is an emptiness that isn't there,
But that holds the rest in a kind of desperate embrace
Until the rest is still, and the loneliness reverberates
With the breathing of an almost human kind of peace.
But the contentment is imaginary, and the tenderness,
Like the tree in God's mind, a figment of contemplation.

The feeling alters or the memory wanes, leaving the mind
Still waiting aimlessly, in the light trance of time,
While the incidents shine on a receding screen,
Or a remark hangs, or some impulse lingers unfulfilled
While love fades, until only a deep difference lasts.
Sometimes at night, when the past opens and the buried
Longings wrap themselves in colors, it almost starts
To seem as though another form of life were possible:
That although anger and love are real, the smaller,
Transitory emotions are real too, and more alive.
Day brings a sense of distance and the schematic moods

Of the depicted life—vacuity, release, and friction,
But behind the friction and the pretense of indifference,
A conception of life as infinitely far away. And the sense
Is sharper, the imagination unrelenting in its isolation,
Yet sometimes, after a walk on a fine morning or a quiet
Meal in the little restaurant, absorbed, for a moment,
In the fleeting pleasures of the afternoon.

2.

Somewhere in the initial, lost experience of fiction
There is a phase of detachment, a dense, irrational
Feeling of enchantment mingled with a sense of loss
So abstract that it must have made the differences
Between memory and the imagination seem almost unreal.
Life wanders or the mind strays, but the story holds,
With the flat, incantatory tones embodying the desire
For consecrated moments and the need for repetition
In the same reflexive images, but becoming stranger,
Until they start to seem something like other people,
Or like figures in some stylized tableau set vaguely
On a coast in midsummer, with the sun shining madly
And the houses strung like pearls above an azure sea.

He was sitting on the terrace with a group of friends,
Lost in another of those vacant, sentimental reveries
About aging and the afternoon, or about how intricately
The summer day ends, or about clothes, or about light.
Along the beach a few waves moved, as the summer people
Watched the gulls descend in slow, exhilarating glides.
Now and then he made a desultory remark, just to amuse,
But his mind was elsewhere, quietly contemplating some
Provisional conception of himself, paradoxically young,
But with some of the details rendered slightly indistinct
By too much passive sensation, and the bright, distracted
Conversation getting more private every year from an excess
Of gin and sun, yet the overall bearing marvelously alert,
Even in repose: the delicate, angular head, rich-old, with

Light, dry hair and eyes that lock and suddenly look away;
The thin, impeccable English shirting; the expensive skin.

He was forty-eight, and still waiting for somebody to adore
Without wanting, or without the ultimate possibility of loss.
His life felt as though it were always just about to start
Or end, or about to become relatively clear; but for now,
Temporary alliances would do, and the minor moods that last
All afternoon, waiting upon the mild exigencies of summer,
Rehearsing the fashionable despondencies, or trashing N.
He was all alone, with a range of sympathy unable to extend
Beyond the glass sphere of consciousness, where he lived
In an illusion of the complacency he'd always wanted, like
A dreamer clinging tightly to what he doesn't have anymore,
Or the mind instinctively reflecting what it can't become.
And then gradually it started to slip away, leaving him
Like someone in his own imagination, fabricating his past,
Breathing in the fragrance of depleted rage and each day
Looking forward helplessly, in perplexity or pain, until
He was beyond forgetting. But he kept it for a while, like
The love he'd held in his hands, then lost in wealth and
Memory abandoned it to tenderness, to the magnification
Of feeling, and to the solitary pretense of regret.

He continued to inhabit his imagination, but with a sharp
Sensation of the way time passes, while its illusion lasts.
He began to think of his life as an interminable preparation
Cast in the form of a reminiscence, with an extended part
In the present tense intended for the contemplation of those
Light boats, and with a phase of indifference followed by a

Sense of exhaustion and a perfunctory ending, for that was
How, eventually, his own renaissance was going to come:
Not in a flood of inspiration, but through an interval of
Change so long that it was going to feel like the meticulous
Development of one constant theme. And then one day
He realized he'd lost the past. There wasn't any
Inevitability anymore, and the imaginary differences
That used to seem so final didn't matter now—
There was just life, but part of his soul was dead
And the rest was waiting in the garden, where a little
Breeze rustled the paper lanterns. Maybe later a
Kind of character would emerge, but that would have
To be in the imagery of another life: the vague,
Abstract affairs, and the distracted way
Love swept the ruins; the play of conversation
And sunlight on a tessellated floor;
The buried stairs.

3.

                    Deep inner dark
Where the violence gleams and the indifferent
Face that only God sees looks up from the water
With its relentless smile, while its features shatter
And float away and its lineaments start to disintegrate
Into shimmering light and dark passages, which one day
Were going to come to seem like elements of happiness.
Sometimes the fragments can illuminate the enormity of the years
And how the soul is lost in them, as in a form of memory
In which there aren't any disillusionments or dreams,
But where it can be seen in its entirety, in an impersonal perspective
And without feeling, or lifted out of its isolated context
Like an inert thing and suspended there until the vertigo subsides
And the illusion that the years converge on it returns.
In dreams, or in these moments of distraction that derive from
      dreams,
Sometimes the waiting can begin to seem so real that the illusion
      fades
Into the security of home, as though everyone else had gone
While the night-light had continued burning, and the future
Had been transformed into an infinite field of possibility again.
Yet in that closed, capacious chamber where his real soul
Inhabited its shadowy mythology of light and recollection,
Delusive memories and self-fulfilling expectations glowed and
      disappeared
In the darkness where he waited patiently, held spellbound
By his mirror image, and by the years collapsing inward in concentric
      waves.

For the past was over, and tomorrow had dwindled to a pin,
While the person in the water had gradually become as alien to him
As the sound of his own voice, as though the characteristic words
Were being spoken by a stranger, in a language he couldn't comprehend
As he listened to the grandiose and convoluted explanation
Without any real sense of understanding, captivated by the air of
    intellect
And the inverted anger, glaring down at the deserted surface
In abject despondency, yet finally acquiescing in its flat,
Fastidious music, with its insistent undertone of sadness
And its persistent tendency towards abstraction, like a fallacious
Argument against the disenchantment that was going to come
Eventually, in the amorphous future, when the twin spells
Would loosen and their two trajectories would intersect.

It's milder now. Summer is ending with the human imagery
Strewn everywhere like fragmentary objects, exhausted by his dreams
And shattered by the sublimated intensity of his actual desires.
And it gets easier to see, yet the rest is still almost impossible to
    understand
Completely, as their faces vanish like despondent ghosts
Into the thin air of consciousness, while the secondary voices
Sleeplessly repeat the customary sanctifying consolations
In their private language, leaving, at the center of the imagination
Just a blank expanse where people merely illustrate each other,
Featureless and flat. But then none of them were real.
It was a waste of feeling, though the aspiration mattered
For its vision of the separate sense of life it would have made
As tangible as the slow hallucination of a summer day.
For he was something more and less than a mirage, a hollow

Simulacrum of that hidden world of feeling and resentment
Where the mind creates its own peculiar history, and its way of
    looking
Back upon itself as through a stranger's eyes, as through a mirror.
And the result is free, like the animula that flourishes in solitude,
Or in that cave of recollection where the colors coalesce
Behind the doppelgänger's death mask, hovering out of reach
    somewhere beyond
The range of consciousness, as though the soul were just a story
    something told
Whose spell was memory and whose quiet theme the deepening sense
    of isolation
Memory brings, until the years begin to seem like stages
Life goes through while love deteriorates and disappears
Into a state of feeling, and then a phase of play and introjection,
Abnegation and exculpatory gestures, and finally into a subjective
    scream.
But he was an idea, and only an idea can dissolve this way,
Like God, into the mystery of someone else. And only in
The guise of a reflection can the soul's intense immediacy be
    apprehended,
Freed from its prison of personality and the contingencies of
    character
Into a condition beyond certainty, in which nothing changes
And it remains alone, in an oblique kind of happiness,
Bathed in the furious transparency that separates it from
Another person's dense, unimaginable interior reality.

4.

Time passes, as a cold wind sweeps the summer shapes away
At the release of autumn, while the intervals between the years
Become shorter, and the illusion of their real significance
Becomes more and more attenuated, and finally disappears.
I used to think that everyone's life was different, and that nobody
    could change
Except by dying, or by gradually withdrawing from the world
Into the mind of God, into the fantasy of being seen for what he was
Objectively, by someone else, in solitude. Day after day
The portrait becomes vaguer as the mind disintegrates,
Yet the essential core of secrecy remains, and the strange sensation
That this sense of life I thought that other people knew so well is
    mine alone.
The illusion is depth. The banality at the heart of things
In which the heart can rest and let its final feelings form
Lies on the surface, and the transitory moods that seemed to deepen
    into life
Vanish like wishes now, like words. What remains behind
Is a kind of feeling of contingency, a gradual waning of the present
Into a mere possibility, as though it were a dream of the extent of life
In which there wasn't any tangible experience of finitude, only a dull,
Unfocused anger as the words slide off the page and out of memory,
And the faces wash away like caricatures on a wall, and the sky fades.
I sometimes think of writing as a way of effacing people, of
    transforming them into ideas
By way of saving them, or of restoring them to that abstract state of
    innocence
From which the burden of the concrete personality descends.

Like sounds in sleep, unreal beyond the confines of their dream,
This force of life beyond intelligence maintains its surge,
But with a separate person cloistered in each moment like eternity,
Cut off from others by the wall of consciousness and from itself by
Time, the form of consciousness, as though to exist at all
Were to remain alone. And yet I'd wanted to remain still
And let the light of recollection flow around me like the gradual
Absolution of the world by darkness, on the verge of sleep.
The common sense of things intensifies, and then dissolves away,
Until a fear of something deep within myself, inert and old,
Is what I have to live in, and the tone of my own voice all I can hear.
What happened to the winds that used to blow from nowhere?
But it flows in one direction, and the imagery that used to seem
    transparent
Is part of its history now, like the dead leaves of fiction,
And the passages that glowed with inner life give back the blank,
Insensate stare that means their intimations of another form of life
    were meaningless.
I know the inside of one story, yet the incessant ache that
Saturates its pages speaks to no one, and its nuances of
Light and thought and feeling aren't reflections of the real
Person who exists and changes, but of the bare soul alone—
Because by starting from another person's life and going on from there
I'd thought, that way, I'd come to feel the difference more deeply;
And because I'd wanted this to be something other than a poem.
This is all there is. And the year has come around again,
The days are longer and the high, thin clouds that gather in the
    atmosphere
Like afterthoughts inside the nearly empty mind don't seem as strange
    now

As they did a little while ago, before my fear of finding no one had
    abated
And the waiting started that has come to seem like happiness,
A condition of mere being, of year to year inhabiting the same
Repetitive illusion until now I feel suspended in its single thought,
As though my world had finally dwindled down to this and left me
    here.

And as the years go by these remnants of a future I once had
Are also going to fade and my indifference deepen; yet somehow the
    mind,
Even in abstraction, seems bound to go on issuing its faint,
Disruptive cries of disagreement that conceal it as it turns away,
Distracted by the sense of something real and unattainable
That I know now is going to characterize my life until I die.
It's not so bad though: no one remembers what the world was actually
    like
On those first evenings, and the poetry that comes and goes
Eradicates all trace of their implicit promises that God was listening
And that time was going to answer in agreement; and it doesn't matter
That instead of being happy I am merely older, for the same
Impatience with myself that brought this private dream to life
Will surely vanish with it, leaving me alone inside a stranger
World than I remember, without any inkling of its underlying
Emptiness, or of having lived here in a kind of wordless paradise
Where nothing changes, now that everything has changed.

The Waiting Game

It is another form of play, one based on partially
Forgotten moods with names that whisper their designs
Until the outside world assumes an air of unreality
That makes it hard to concentrate; with once again an
Odd sensation, as of someone staring in at commonplace
Realities arranged against a background of confusing,
Tentative emotions twisted in the mind until they break
As a sob breaks, and lines go streaming down the pane.
They come to me alone, at first amorphous and serene, in
Sighs and platitudes against a faint interior refrain,
Or awkwardly, in syllables that lurch, and then in lucent,
Plangent tones distilled from some obscure uneasiness,
Like vagrant moods restored to sense, that ebb and flow
In fluent, captivating motions paralleling those in dreams.
Sometimes they seem to me no more or less than convoluted
Variations on a single mode of being, phrased in narrow terms
Dictated by exaggerated feelings splayed across a large,
Pretentious canvas on the ostentatious scale of the unseen;
But also bare and plain, almost as though their subtlest
Gradations, shadings, and obscurities might finally be
Contained in a transparent breath, or in a casual remark
Between two complex sentences, like warm fall rain.

I want the rain to wash these sentiments away,
Leaving their average core exposed, their variegated
Fabric smooth and visible again. Whatever permanence
They have is one of attitudes, as in those long, imaginary
Games we used to play on distant summer evenings when the

Light was simple and its affirmation clear and never ending.
Why can't these artless forms of meaning actually exist?
I wish there were a simple way to write about emotions,
Even indirectly, leaving the texture of the words intact,
Yet with the full intensity of hate or happiness or sorrow.
I wish there were a form of feeling with the elementary
Feeling of the body, eloquent and ample in its unawareness,
Without any notion of tomorrow, or of something lying in wait.
I say these things, although I recognize their futility,
Because of the uncertain weight and character and shape my
Own emotions have come to have for me. I want to focus back
To where the vagueness started, grasping them again with an
Evasive understanding that comes later, living them again
Vicariously, through a persuasive song of solitude whose
Certainty is indirection, and whose faint misgivings are a
Silent introspection and a passion for the insubstantial,
Lending it a dense air of substance, yet giving it as well
An ordinary sense of life, though one resembling nothing
Tangible beyond the long, elaborate breath of dying.

Between the Lines

The thoughts came, and then eventually the
Words that made those thoughts seem weightless.
I stepped aside to let the voice flow, barely
Conscious of myself or my relation to its sound.
Somewhere the birds sang, but I couldn't see them
And their song remained remote in its indifference
To the things around me, while the things around me
Melted into language, leaving me essentially alone,
And yet enveloped in this perfect form of happiness.
It was like leaving home—the world I'd come to know
Became imaginary and dissolved into the background,
While its place was taken by a totally different one,
Oblivious to my own, yet just as intricate and real.
"Come in," a voice said. "I've been waiting for you."
And I found the room where I have waited half my life
For someone else to enter, for my statement to be done
And for this disaffected life to be completed. My days
Pass quietly, and at night I reassemble them in dreams.
I spend my time infatuated with a grandiose illusion,
Captivated by these things that speak to me in words
Reverberating with a vague and unarticulated fear that
There is too much here, too much for me to understand.

Sometimes I think that I can feel the outside world
Relax, and feel its weight become a part of me again.
The thoughts that linger in the mind, the sounds that
Filter through the trees—these things aren't merely
Signs of some imaginary life to be denied me while the

Heart of everything I used to have remains alive. It
Troubles me that time should make things sweeter, that
Instead of learning to perceive things as they are I've
Learned to lose them, or to see them as they disappear
Into the insubstantial future. Everything here is mine,
Or lies within my power to accept. I want to find a way
To live inside each moment as it comes, then let it go
Before it breaks up in regret or disillusionment. I've
Constantly defined myself by difference, yet after all
These years I feel as far away as ever from the kind of
Strength I'd hoped the differences would bring. Where
Is that boundless life I know exists beyond the words?
When will the fear that makes me cling to them be gone
And leave me undivided? I can hear the transitory song
The birds sing, but what dominates my mind remains the
Faint, insistent one that draws me back into this dim
Interior where something waits for me, and waits alone.

So I've remained here, in a place where no one comes
And I can hear the voice and visualize the image of a
Person with his heart grown tired, his soul diminished
By the struggle to maintain itself against the world.
Perhaps someday I'll recognize that voice as mine and
Come to see that figure as my own; or leave the ghosts
Behind and take my place as part of the surroundings.
Right now I float above the line that separates the
Two perspectives from each other and divides my life.
A future is emerging in the distance. Is it mine, or
Merely one I've dreamed about? Life flows around me
While my own remains unchanged by the advancing years,

As faces I can't recognize appear and disappear and
Come at last to rest. Is this how one survives? In
Someone else's memory? My soul is all but gone but
Where? I know that what is left will keep a minor
Part of me alive by just existing—either as this
Thing that by the force of sheer despair begins to
Move and breathe and then to turn away from here
And stare into the world and see it whole, yet
Distantly; or else as something that remains
Beside itself, and paralyzed with fear.

Threnody for Two Voices

—This is my complaint: that
Humiliation in the snow. I've carried it
This far, made hate so much a part of me
The past seems riddled with despair, and my life hurts,
And the words that find me curl up at the edges.
You keep asking me where, and yet I see it everywhere,
I see it here at home: in the arguments after dinner
And the tense confinement of the living room; the sudden
Ringing of the telephone; the anger that wells up in me each morning.
I feel it in my bones. This secret life
Whose language is the melancholy sound the heart makes
Beating against its cage—why can't you feel the
Emptiness I see reflected in your face, why can't you
Sense this overwhelming thing I have no name for?
The present is a dull, persistent ache, the future an impersonal expanse
In which I'm tentative and old, and my life has come to nothing.
I want to keep the emptiness away, to realize the
Sense of what it's like to be alive—instead of just existing
In a frozen atmosphere of rage, where the thoughts go
Swirling through my mind like snowflakes.

—Yes. And yet some days seemed different.
I remember the enchantment and the peaceful light
That used to settle on the yard on summer evenings.
Couldn't some of that return? My world feels broken,
And the world that you describe is one that I can't see,
In which there isn't any happiness, and where the sky became
Opaque and lost its tenderness, and what had seemed like

Poetry became two separate monologues, imprisoning each of us in
    a name.
Why can't the truth be like a dream from which two people can wake
    up and kiss?
Why can't our separate lives share *this* illusion:
Rounded by contentment and well-being, infinite and free
And yet at peace within the boundaries of our life
Together, in a language that contains us like a shell?
I don't know—perhaps there isn't any peace
And everything I say is futile. Maybe we're alone
And what you say is merely confirmation, further proof
That all that lies between the poles of solitude and death
Is the rhetoric of loss, of feeling cheated by a world
That whispered quietly of love and left us with this incoherent
Thing that love has brought us to despise.

—The truth is smaller. What you mean by love
Isn't anything I recognize. You mean a style of contemplation,
Or a monument encapsulating everything you cling to
Like a first certainty—things which to me are merely
Emblems of obscurity and death: the hurt bewilderment;
Your maddening inability to see; your breathless concentration
And these rambling explanations filled with a grandiose
Self-pity and a sadness on the scale of the universe.
What's missing is the dailiness, the commonplace
Engagements that could make this formal universe a home.
I had the thought that what was called a "normal" life
Was really a form of cruelty, and that the people who could stand it
    lived in hell.
One time I even thought you might agree with me,

And come to me in my head, and start to understand me.
It doesn't matter now. What matters are these syllables
That shape the endless argument in which we live.
Is this the peace you bring me? I hover between two minds
As in an endless space, I feel my body drift through
All-consuming layers of anxiety, still harboring a wish
That you might cling to me, and then let me go.

—I know that I can bring you nothing but my own
Uneasy mix of insight and illusion, and a voice that
Beckons like a distant singing in the trees, and no delight.
I think that what might free you is the effortless
Forbearance which I haven't the capacity to give. To
Rest in peace, inspired by the simple breath of happiness;
To remain indifferent to the frame of one's existence—
These aren't compelling ways to live. Life has to hold the
    consciousness of death,
Or it isn't life, but something featureless. This
Thing you call your soul is just the music of a solitary quest
Inexorably approaching, through layers of frustrated magic,
The dead core. It sings more clearly in the air, more
Urgently in the darkness, floating through the bare trees,
Coursing with the thrill of anger through the veins . . .
My song is simpler: disappointment, and the pain of isolation,
And the hope that something in its underlying tenderness
Might still appease you, might approach you in a calm and
Restless voice that sings more sweetly as the summer wanes;
And still more silently in autumn, as the grave opens
And the earth makes ready to receive its guest.

    ◆ ◆

—And sets me free. For did you think that all the
Force of my conviction, all the strength of my prolonged
    dissatisfaction,
Might amount to nothing? That what started as a way of
Fighting back the emptiness I felt encroaching on my heart
Might be simply in vain? I can't go back to that romantic
Wilderness again, in which my passions felt like questions
And my dreams were private motions in a universe of one.
This impasse may be lasting. It may ultimately heal.
What matters is that something in my soul began to breathe
As I began to see your words as merely part of my experience,
And to feel that almost none of what they said to me was true.
What freedom means to me is not depending on the world,
Or on you, or on some fantasy to tell me how to live. It's
Not enough to mirror my despair, and give it back to me.
I want to see myself as what I am, and look at you the way
    you are—
Is that a form of hatred? Or an intricate form of care
That lets another person be? Or a form of self-deception
Leaving both of us alone, but with our disparate lives
Uneasily together at the end, within a blank and
Intimate expanse? Maybe now you see.

Un Autre Monde

The nervous style and faintly reassuring
Tone of voice concealed inside the meanings
Incompletely grasped, and constantly disappearing
As the isolated moments burst against each other
And subside—these are the aspects left behind
Once the sense is over, and the confusion spent.
They belong to the naive, perennial attempt to see
And shift the focus of experience, fundamentally
Revising what it means to feel, yet realizing
Merely some minor, disappointing alterations
In the fixed scheme of things. I bring to it
Nothing but bare need, blind, continual obsession
With the private way life passes into nothing
And a mind as fragile as a heart. It started out
Indifferently but soon became my real way of feeling,
Abstract tears, an anger retrospectively revealing
Darker interpretations of the fears that filled me to
Exploding, ill-defined desires, vague anxieties and
Satisfactions that were once so much a part of me
I miss them, and I want them back. And yet in time
They did come back as wishes, but the kind of wishes
Long ago abandoned, left behind like markers on the way
To resignation, and then as infinitely fine regrets,
And then as aspects of some near, receding world
Inert as yesterday, and no longer mine.

A Perspective Box

for Douglas Crase and Frank Polach

Sometimes the desert almost comes alive for me again
In a reprise of home, tracing a perspective line that
Steadily flows away in an unmemorable progression of
Ineffable, plain moments making up the individual life
Shaped like my own, taken from some ephemeral tomorrow
Indistinctly seen, in a barren landscape of dry flowers
And distant mountains floating in the vacant heat, yet
Visibly at hand, on an afternoon now torn away from me,
And which gradually has become, like once-dense hours
Drained of their intuitions, little more than a memory
Of the kind that brings back nothing beyond some vague
Uncertainties of feeling and the brute facts of sense;
As the seasons wrap their stereotypes around the mind
—Thin, transparent spring, and summer with its chores
And colors—and the vagaries of time remain endless.

I often dream of gravitating back across that timeless
Adolescent landscape when, in the inert light of dawn,
Another, older light begins to filter back to me again,
Its gentle illumination flooding the interior recesses
Of a private world one mind alone can understand.
The road leads downward through the incandescent haze
Into that mental wilderness where space abruptly ends
And time lies sleeping; where you can feel a daylight
Sensibility give way to something infinitely clearer,

With its animating gaze turned inward towards a view
No longer visible, yet here in yesterday's uncharted,
Inaccessible confusion, where the land, brooding and
Unknown, continues to exist; and even yet more deeply
Here in my own heart, whose unseen passages still roam
Through those imaginary hills above the valley floor.

There is a simple view that writes away pure presence
As a kind of visionary feeling, one of loss. Diffused,
Its elemental glow reduced to mere reflections of some
Disembodied fantasies or dreams, the country I remember
Is a cipher to me, worn away by distance and the years
Into part of my mind, as though the real world beyond a
Shifting vantage point of temperament and place and time
Were an illusion. For me the desert remains the emblem
Of sheer consciousness, a clear feeling, in that vibrant
Furnace air, of the anomalous fact of sentient existence
And, concealed by a bare horizon, of the enormous future
Which has become today, in which everything merely *seems*
And memories caress the place names—*Julian* and *Cuyamaca*,
Caliente, *Vallecito*, and *El Centro*—as they remain there
At the level of enchantment, without engaging the real.

Where *is* the real? A few weeks ago I drove back there,
Riding out of my imagination through the same impassive
Mountains that I drove through years ago, then steeply
Down into an intact, empty plain, where only desiccated
Syllables remained of those immensities I used to feel
Reflected my soul; then back to what was left of home
And the diluted world I live in, with the quiet motion

Intermittently portraying, on a minuscule scale, these
Late, distracted moments into which eternity intrudes.
I enjoy these days—I like their even, uneventful line
Stretching in both directions—and yet they seem to me
Too literal, their dazzling prospect rendered visible
In retrospect, but the view essentially the same, only
More limited, and the landscape less and less extreme
As it leads back home, and then relentlessly away.

The Advent of the Ordinary

I hadn't thought of it like this at all. I saw,
Or like to think I saw, a different kind of life
—An undivided one—detached from its surroundings,
Yet at peace within them; separate from the world
Reflected in its own unbroken mirror, yet entirely
Inhabiting a space that I could recognize as mine.
Outside was chaos, but the minutes flowed together
So discreetly time was nonexistent, leaving me with
Nothing to decipher or define. I heard someone sigh,
And then, within the sigh, a premonition of myself as
Finally emerging from a narcissistic dream into this
Bland, anonymous condition. *Is this mine? Is this*
The liberation that was going to come to me? I felt
Alone, but at the center of some infinite potential
Time and time alone would realize, with an expanding
Sense of what it meant to be alive, and with a soul
Whose powers of understanding grew in my imagination—
Deeper and more stark—until at last it almost seemed
That I could visualize my life and see it whole; yet
All I saw were different ways of being human, mute
Misshapen memories, and pieces of my heart, combined
Within the compass of a love whose form was darkness.
I felt its shape move in slow motion, felt its voices
Echoing my heart. I tried to dream away my life, to
Pare the skin away and then, like something undefined,
Float free from circumstance, then down these narrow
Passageways and alleys, moving through them with an
Ambling gait whose tempo varied with my mood. Beyond

My dream the world unrolled as usual, distantly. I
Let its noise flow through me unimpeded, let my mind
Erase those outward images that passed before my eyes
As in a magic-lantern show reflecting everything I'd
Cared about or seen; I let my thoughts turn inside out
Until they glittered in a kind of space. I pushed it
Farther, made the sights seem arbitrary, made the pace
Like that of walking through a foreign city, lurching
As the streets passed and the sea swam into view. I
Felt its breeze on my face, heard someone's breathing
Gradually subsiding. Then I came back to this life.

What the Stars Meant

On a backwards-running clock in Lisbon,
By the marble statue of Pessoa;
On an antique astrolabe in London
Tracing out the sky above Samoa,

Thousands of miles away—in time, in place,
Each night conspires to create a myth
That stands for nothing real, yet leaves you with
The vague impression of a human face.

The fragments fly apart and shift, trembling
On the threshold of a kind of fullness:
The minor wonder of remembering;
The greater wonders of forgetfulness.

For one looks back as someone else might yearn
For a new life, and set his course upon
The polestar, bid his adieus, and move on.
The journey takes a solipsistic turn,

Forsaking starlight for an inner glow,
And reducing all human history,
All human culture—highbrow, middle, low—
To one reflecting surface, one story.

What fills the heaven of a single mind?
The things that used to fill Kant's mind with awe

—"The starry heavens and the moral law"—
Seem distant now, and difficult to find

Amid the message of satiety
Issuing from the corners of the sky,
Filled with monotonous variety:
Game shows, an interview with Princess Di,

And happy talk, and sitcoms and the news,
The shit that floats across your living room
Each weekday evening. Waiting in the pews,
Out in the desert where the cacti bloom,

Something else was forming, something stranger
Gathering in the gulf below the stairs—
As though the mystery of the manger
Were written in the day-to-day affairs

Of a world consecrated to Mammon,
Yet governed by those sacred absences
That make the spirit soar, and presences
At one remove, like the sound of Cuban

Drumbeats issuing from the Ricardos'
Love nest on the television station
Like distant thunder; or Leonardo's
"Wave that flees the site of its creation."

◆ ◆

In the desert far beyond the city,
One hears the cadences for which one longs,

The lyrics of those half-forgotten songs
—Some of them poignant, some of them witty—

Brimming with the melody of passage;
One feels the wind that blows the soul about,
Repeating its inscrutable message;
And as night falls, one sees the stars come out.

I found myself beneath a canopy
Of scenes left out of someone else's life
—The dog that didn't bark, Rosebud, Cain's wife—
Arrayed above me in a panoply

Of glittering debris, gigantic swirls
Of stars, and slowly moving caravans
Of stars like tiny Christmas lights or pearls
Of tapioca, floating in a Danse

Macabre across the heavens as I stood,
Watching the pageant in the sky unfold.
I felt the chill of something much too old
To comprehend—not the Form of the Good,

But something inchoate and violent,
A Form of Darkness. Suddenly the songs
Floating through the revelry fell silent,
As in *The Masque of the Red Death*, as throngs

Of the dead twinkled at me from above.
The intimate domain of memory

Became an endless field of entropy
Transfigured, inking in the outlines of

Eurydice entombed, Orpheus immured,
And, in the center of their universe,
That subtler diadem of stars obscured
By the brighter constellations, the Hearse.

Standing off to one side, as though bereft,
There was a figure with averted eyes,
Gesturing in a language of surprise
That took possession of my heart, yet left

The question of her meaning unresolved.
I looked at her. It was time to begin.
The apparations in the sky dissolved,
Leaving me alone, and growing old. In

The wide, unstructured heavens overhead
The stars were still shining. When I got home,
The message light was blinking on the phone.
I don't remember what the message said.

The Constructor

They strike me less as actual persons than as abstract
Ghosts of an idea: that life is the external part of
Its emotions, of the small, evaporating sentiments; but
That in isolation there might be a place where you could
Live eternally behind the high, intimidating walls of art.
They knew that in the end the parts were unimportant—that
Even as the world receded language fell away until the body
Shook with feeling and became intangible; that eventually
One's soul would be absorbed by its surroundings, breath by
Simplifying breath, advancing towards that moment when its
Work would be completed and its past restored, as though
Swept forward on a quiet, undulating wave of meaning, and
As in a trance. And so they floated through their lives,
Protected by the great, exhausted themes of the romantics:
That understanding lay in childhood; that in emancipated
Language one possessed a real way of merging opposites, of
Joining the discursive tone of reason with the weight of the
Emotions to create a finite, earthly music; that any person,
By a simple act of will, could meld the substance of his life
And the seclusion of the mind together in a single testament
Suffused with light and feeling and reverberating with the
Fundamental rhythms of the heart, and never break the spell.
But those ideas are shells now, empty as those stories of the
Soul inhabiting its lost utopia—that bright, fictitious era
When a glance could take it in, a word could start it, and
The merest touch could lead it backwards through the narrow
Ways of the imagination to a paradise of innocence and peace.
Sometimes I feel this hollow sense of satisfaction at their

Disappearance, at the loss of that seductive power to make
A world seem real and bring one's individual fantasies to
Life; but other times I feel like someone living in a fable
Of his own construction, waiting in some bleak, completely
Isolated country with no hope or history, where the minutes
Come and go and memories displace each other, leaving nothing
For the soul to do but feel them as they flow, and flow away.
I know the forms of care, and understand the grammar of desire.
I understand that life is an affair of words, and that the
Hope of duplicating it is a delusion. There is a mood that
Drains it of significance, reducing all its aspirations to
A single state of mind, and all its tenderest emotions to
An empty sense of self-importance fostered by the primitive
Confusions of some distant place and time. Is this how life
Was meant to feel? For this is how, increasingly, it does.
You *want* there to be something more than just these tedious
Realities of disillusionment and anxiousness and care, and
Then you see them rising in the distance, luminescent forms
Ascending from these categorical expressions of unmeaning
In a curve that sweeps up like the graph of an obsession.
More and more their presence comes to dominate your dreams
At night, or linger in the corner of your mind by day. You
Close your eyes and something filters into consciousness;
You try to read, but with a sense of someone watching you.
One time I'd thought they'd gone away, but gradually they
Reappeared, permeating the surrounding atmosphere with
Music swirling in and all around me like a deep refrain.
And for a while they almost seem about to welcome you, to
Show you into their imaginary garden and to tell you how
Life felt, and how the world appeared before it started:

44

Everything melts away, until in place of the familiar,
Inessential background you begin to see the image, slowly
Coming in and out of focus, of a face you never saw before,
As though behind this wall of words there were a solitary
Presence with an unfamiliar name and with the abstract,
Heightened features of a ghost. And then the noise stops
And the language disappears, and the semblance on the page
Stares blindly back at you until it almost starts to seem
That there might be a vision of yourself that real too—
A vision of the soul, or God, or something merely human
That could live forever with the strength of an illusion.
But when I turn away and look I see myself, by contrast,
As a purely local person, temporal, not quite complete,
Unequal to the numinous desires that brought them back to
Earth and made their world seem new again, and beautiful.
I want to feel things burst again, to read life as it was
Before its truth became apparent and its youth had faded
And the doors closed on the future. I wait here in the
Narrow dispensations of the moments, mired in a state of
Vague anticipation, working through the days as through
The pages of a schoolbook, drifting through these subtly
Recursive grammars of the heart by rote, in fragments,
As though suspended in the first, uncertain stages
Of some distant happiness; in private terms and notes
That show myself to me, but which create a personality
Half-Ariel, half-real, that lives in phrases, and whose
Animus is word association, mingling those things it
Might have been with those that one can't see or even
Consciously imagine. One gets resigned to them, but
In the way the blind become resigned to the invisible,

Or the mind to finitude. One becomes sufficient. One
Even finally attains—though only at the level of the
Personal—an empty kind of freedom, mired in disbelief,
Beset by contradictory feelings, looking back at them
Sometimes in awe, and with a sense of the impossible,
Sometimes in anger; now and then in gratitude. Yet
Now and then I find myself methodically rehearsing
One or two stock narratives, and one or two ideas,
In unadorned, discursive terms and cadences that
Seem to be inspired by the breath of God, by waves
Of silent, urgent sound proliferating through and
All around me, as the past, like some mysterious
Ventriloquist, announces them in enigmatic ways.
And then I feel a part of their confusion, and at
One with them in aspiration, sharing those desires
That fostered their illusion of a poetry of stark,
Unmediated passion that revealed the soul directly;
And their faith in its redemption through a reckless,
Youthful art, begun in gladness as a kind of refuge
From the never-ending disappointments of the ordinary,
And as solace for its fall from grace into the human.
Was that all unreal? Another obsolescent exercise in
Self-delusion, nurtured in the heart and now exhausted?
Life is what you call it, but I find no words for it
In what it has become, a language emptied of its vanity
And echoing a truer rhetoric, but a despondent one:
That the burden of a poem is to recall it to itself;
That what was said and done is all there is, and that
There are no further heavens—not even earthly ones—
Beyond the ambiguities of what actually existed; that

The notion of the soul, and reaching out in desperation
For another one, are merely versions of the beautiful;
And that the present is a prison and the past a wall.
Yet once I thought I sensed a different way of feeling,
One of bare simplicity, a respite from these solitary,
Powerful abstractions and these melodramas of the mind.
I thought I felt a moment opening like an unseen flower
Only to close again, as though something else had called it,
Or as though, beneath the disaffected surface, something
Limpid and benevolent were moving at a level of awareness
I could not yet find; and so I let the moment slide away.
One reaches back in eagerness, but in an empty exercise,
For what one might have done. One reads the histories
Of art and solitude for what they say about tomorrow,
And deciphers the illusions of the past for what they
Might illuminate about today, for they were once alive.
One tries to penetrate the different dreams of reason
Buried in their tablatures, to translate the universal
Language of their faces and the outward aspects of a
Finite, inner universe. Why is it that as one gets
Closer their incredible diversity reduces to a smooth,
Impregnable facade? Whatever else their codes might
Show or say—a mood, a moment, or a whole cosmology—
Their private meaning is a person, and it fades away
As page by page or note by note one comes to hear the
Novel's ending, not the soul that wrote it, or to hear
The music of a dead composer, not a living one; and
Then to see them as emotions that in time, or someplace
After time, might gradually give way to something real.
Why must there be so many ways to disillusionment, of

Coming to believe that no one else can feel and that
One really *is* alone? Sometimes I feel like nothing in
This world or any other one, now like an exile,
Now a subject of the kingdom of the inconceivable.
I wanted to look past them into what their world was
Like before they finally called it home, before there
Was a state of nature to ascend from, or a pretext for
These differences I feel. I tried to kid myself that
I could talk to them directly, mixing their traditions
With the vague one of my own to conjure the imaginary
Figure of these songs without a context; carefully
Constructing one in long, erotic sentences expressing
An unfocused state of sadness, one whose proof remained
Inviting and unknown; phrasing their encouragements
Too reasonably; fashioning their reassurances that
Someday soon my time was going to come, but meanwhile
Rearranging things to make them more believable, and
Going through the sweet, hypnotic motions of a life.
There was this chorus of strange vapors, with a name
Something like mine, and someone trying to get free.
You start to see things almost mythically, in tropes
And figurations taken from the languages of art—to
See your soul as sliding out of chaos, changeable,
Twice blessed with vagueness and a heart, the feelings
Cumbersome and unrefined, the mood a truly human one
Of absolute bewilderment; and floating up from that
To an inanimate sublime, as though some angel said
Come with me, and you woke into a featureless and
Foolish paradise your life had gradually become; or
From a dense, discordant memory into a perfect world

As empty as an afterthought, and level as a line.
One day a distant cloud appears on the horizon, and
You think your life might change. These artifacts,
Whose temper mirrors mine, still argue with the same
Impersonal intensity that nothing personal can change;
And yet one waits. Where did the stark emotions go,
Where are the flowers? Mustn't there be something to
This tenderness I feel encroaching on my mind, these
Quiet intimations of a generous, calm hour insensibly
Approaching day by day through outwardly constricted
Passages confused by light and air? It starts to seem
So effortless, and something slides away into the artless
Afterlife where dreams go, or a part that all along had
Been too close to feel begins to breathe as it becomes
Increasingly transparent, and then suddenly alive.
I think I can at last almost see through them into
Everyday unhappiness, my clear, unhampered gaze
No longer troubled by their opaque atmosphere of
Rational irrationality, their reasonable facade
An ordinary attitude, their sense of consequence
Merely illusory. Why should it matter whether
One or two of them survive? They calm the days
With undirected passion and the nights with music,
Hiding them at first, then gradually revealing them
So differently—these things I'd thought I'd never
Have—simply by vanishing together one by one, like
Breaths, like intermittent glimpses of some incomplete,
Imperfect gratitude. How could this quiet feeling
Actually exist? Why do I feel so happy?

Fleeting Forms of Life

I guess the point is that the
Task would seem that much more
Difficult without the kind of
Peace they bring me, or the

Hope I always find in their
Elaborate denials and evasions,
In these brief, extraordinary
States that settle over me.

They bring an aura of restraint,
Of things interminably delayed, of
Fantasies that organize my nights
And occupy my days with dreams.

I like to think of them as ways
To reinvent myself, as forms that
Constitute a life alternative to
Mine, but that convey a mood I

Realize can seem at times almost
Unreal, almost inhuman, almost
Willfully despondent. True,
I want to rid myself of things

That lent my life its savor,
Like those prospects of a future

That dissolved as I got older,
Or the promises of a past that

Got away somehow; but after that
I want to wake into the years and
Slowly try to recreate my world
By living in it, here and now.

Au Train

I like the view. I like the clear,
Uncompromising light that seems both
Ageless and renewed year after year.
I like the way the wind dies down at
Night until the lake grows still, and
How the fog conceals it in the morning.
I like to feel the breeze come up and
Then to watch the day emerging from the
Sky's peculiar blue, with distant sounds
And subjects magnified as they approach
My mind, and it prepares to take them in.
I know that most of what there is remains
Unseen, unfelt, or subject to indifference
Or change; and yet somehow I find I want to
See things in a way that only renders them
Unreal, and finally as extensions of myself:
To look at them as aspects of my feelings,
As reflections of these transitory moods I
Know are going to fade, or dreams the years
Obliterate; and then to stare into my soul
And try to wish them back again, until they
Look essentially the same—some boats, those
Trees along the shore across the lake, that
Dense horizon line—as though refracted by my
Own imaginary memories. I look at them and
Think of how they must have looked before.
I think of all the forms of happiness, and

How I'd fantasized that it might come to me
In minor moments of transcendence when the
Earth takes on the quality of air, its light
Transformed by that intensely introspective
Gaze that finds its subject in the sky. I
Think of how my heart would start to open,
How some clouds above a tree could seem as
Close to me as leaves, while ordinary sounds
—Like birds, or distant cars—could almost
Feel as though they came from deep within me.
Where did all those feelings go? I have a
Clearer sense of my surroundings, but their
Elemental glow is gone, the mere delusion of
Deliverance seems so far away, and day-to-day
Existence is a burden, dull and full of care.
At times I think I sense it in the distance,
That unnecessary angel by whose grace the
Stones sang and my vagrant heart responded,
That conveyed my waking dreams to earth but
Left them there, confined to what they are,
Yet more than that. And then I find myself
Reflecting things, imagining a vantage point
From which the years will all seem equal, a
Conception of myself and of the world that
Locates them in retrospect and brings their
Conflict to an end. I think I might have
Seen at least some fragments of the truth
Concealed in those imaginary feelings that
Appeared to me in ways I didn't recognize,

That spoke to me in terms of consolation
And that lent me something more than words,
Yet less than wings, and that were simply
Parts of what it meant to be alive.

The Lake of White Flowers

It was a limited ideal,
That made a virtue of its own deficiency:
Dark, inert, and silent at the core,
Yet surrounded by a delicate penumbra of ideas
And sensations jostling one another
In a vague haze of speculation.
It all seemed so effortless and free,
So unconstrained by anything like knowledge
Or the burden of experience. The years to come
Were still unformulated, while their words
Passed like little blips across my mind,
Like a blue sky with a frieze of birds. And
Now they seem like emblems of another age,
An age of acquiescence and discovery,
Filled with interminable conversations,
Interminable nights, and songs like momentary
Blooms that moved from shape to shape
In a mysterious wave that made me happy.
I thought I knew what they meant,
But I didn't know. Poems of knowledge
Speak with accuracy and gravity and grace,
And cast a common shadow. These were lovely
In an incidental way, without magnificence.
But I still think that some of them were true.

A Parking Lot with Trees

A delusion quickly flits away; we easily contrive to make the fantasm, as it were, hate us, because we do not understand what it essentially is.

ROBERT WALSER

This is a fable I conspired to believe.
Its subject is a possibility that may not be my own,
The subject of a fate that wasn't up to me,
Of things I couldn't have foreseen; and how one day I found myself
Alone, contented, more or less alive,
But only vaguely understood—a sort of life
That came to me the way the past came from confusion,
Or the plain necessities of middle age
Descended from the accidents of childhood.
Sometimes I think I'm stranded in myself
The way a character can seem suspended in a story:
As a voice, or as a witness to events—intense or boring,
Actual or unreal—it strings together
In a calm phenomenology of disappointment.
But then the landscape melts away, and the sky
Takes on the character it had when I was younger.
Where is that person whom I took myself to be?
Why has my life been mostly puzzlement, and hope, and inexperience?
Its ghost is humming in the summer haze, and soon another melody
    begins,
And images of dust and sunlight float across my mind
Until I think that I can almost see myself again, this time

Impersonally—suspended in an August afternoon
That ended long ago, in thoughts that shimmered on the verge of
    sense
When worlds collided, or in plain, flat-footed songs
That came to me as random evocations of the past.
For I believed that none of them were accidents at all,
But aspects of a different mode of being that in time might
Yield a glimpse of something wonderful and strange;
And that behind their hidden meaning lay my life.

Sometime in 1953: a memory of a drive-in movie,
Then a view of downtown in the rain. And sometime after that
I find a memory of staring through a magnifying glass
At a dissected frog. But mostly I would dream and read
And migrate in my mind across the country while I
Fantasized about the person I intended to become.
"Life took me by the shoulders, and its wonderful gaze rested on
    mine."
More memories: morning fog, some pastel stucco houses
Built along a canyon, and a campfire in a desert filled with stars.
I know my dreams were no more part of me than anyone's,
And yet in retrospect I like to think that I believed they were.
I like to think that I aspired to the life I'd read about in books,
Of "yellow cocktail music," trains that took you home again and
    bright,
Fantastic mansions filled with rooms that led to other, brighter rooms,
That came to me like Muzak in a vast, deserted
Airport where I waited in the numb hours of the morning.
One year later I looked back at what I'd done
And found it insufficient. I remember going to a movie

Where a man kept dreaming of a clock hand slicing off his head.
I thought that there was time for me to start all over,
To embark upon a program of interior definition
That eventually might yield a quietly spectacular conclusion
(But a private one) against the gradually emerging background of late
Adolescent melodies that hadn't quite begun and
That would soon be over. Cold midwinter sunlight
Slanted through my dormitory window.
A Supreme sang *run, run, run,*
And still each year I looked and felt no older.

Sometimes a life comes true in unexpected ways.
The face that it exhibits to the world appears no different,
While its voice remains essentially the same, and inside even feels the
    same.
Time seems suspended, and the mind feels infinite again.
Meanwhile its song, like someone who has spent his day
Meandering through a meadow, changes course with rapidly increasing
    speed
And plunges headlong down a pathway into darkness.
I came to realize that *I* was what had changed:
That even though I wanted to believe that nothing much had
    happened,
No one knew me anymore, and people I encountered seemed remote
    and strange.
I felt like an increasingly composite individual, in whose name some
Pieces of the person I had been and settings it had wanted to escape
    from
Were combined together. I thought of going back there,

Not to try to pull them back together, but to
Look at them again, because I finally wanted to include them too.
They'd disappeared; there were some highways in the valley,
And a shopping mall where children used to play.
Its features became frightening, while its tone, relaxed and
Confident at first, soon trailed nervously away
Along a meaningless digression. Like a bunch of snapshots,
Each particular seemed clear; only the whole was
Hazy with obscurity and governed by the logic of the moon.
My way of sidling into things had come and gone
And I was getting sick of what I heard: some
Half-remembered monologues whose underlying theme was always
Long, how long, delivered in the still, contorted voice of someone
Constantly alone, and which at best were fragments,
Yet which taken all together made a kind of history
In the quest tradition, one whose disconnected episodes
Receded in a narrative progression that persuaded me of things I'd
    always known.
I wanted to return to where it started: a decaying mill town
With some churches on its corners, and two statues in the square.
All night the raindrops pounded on the roof
While I prepared to try to penetrate its mysteries again
With an emotion that felt something like despair,
Yet with the hope that what had seemed too difficult last night
Might suddenly seem clearer in the morning, like a forest after rain.
I felt compelled by something that I couldn't see,
That whispered from the dark side of the mirror—by an image,
Nourished underneath a rock, of clotted viscera
And blunt, frustrated passions, that propelled me inside out

Along a road that led through danger, over cliffs and mountains
But that ended in a parking lot with trees, where people knew me
And would listen while I told them of the convoluted way I'd come . . .

                              Yet why should they believe me?
And how should I respond? I guess the fantasy took hold too soon,
Before I'd had sufficient time to think it through.
Despite the dreams, those lessons of the night that
Taught me how to live inside its complicated song it
All seems too familiar, like a script someone had written, or a reverie
    I'd planned.
I wish the songs that moved me once might come to me again
And help me understand this person that I've gradually become,
Yet long ago imagined—a perfectly ordinary one
Whose mansion is the future, but whose setting is a
Landscape of a summer afternoon, with a sky heavy in the distance
And a book resting lightly in his hands.

Permissions Acknowledgments

The poems in this book have been published in the following magazines:

The American Poetry Review: "The Advent of the Ordinary"; *Broadway 2:* "The Other Condition"; *Chicago Review:* "What the Stars Meant"; *The Denver Quarterly:* "Au Train"; *The Gettysburg Review:* "The Constructor"; *Gulf Coast:* "Threnody for Two Voices"; *New American Writing:* "A Parking Lot with Trees"; *The New Republic:* "The Lake of White Flowers" and "Sunday Evening"; *Panoply:* "Between the Lines"; *The Paris Review:* "Mistral"; *Private:* "Fleeting Forms of Life"; *Southwest Review:* "The Waiting Game"; *Sycamore Review:* "A Perspective Box"; *TriQuarterly:* "'I Heard a Fly Buzz . . . ,'" "The Saturday Matinee," and "Un Autre Monde"; *The Yale Review:* "Pining Away."

"The Constructor" was reprinted in New Literary History. "Mistral" was reprinted in *Best American Poetry 1988*, John Ashbery and David Lehman, eds. (Scribners). "Pining Away" was translated by Jonathan Galassi and reprinted in Spazio Umano as "Struggersi."

About the Author

John Koethe was born in San Diego, California, on December 25, 1945. He was educated at Princeton and Harvard universities and is Professor of Philosophy at the University of Wisconsin—Milwaukee. He is the author of Blue Vents (Audit/Poetry, Buffalo, 1968); Domes (Columbia, 1973), for which he received the Frank O'Hara Award for Poetry; The Late Wisconsin Spring (Princeton, 1984); and Falling Water (HarperCollins, 1997), for which he received the Kingsley Tufts Poetry Award. He has been the recipient of Guggenheim and NEA fellowships and is also the author of The Continuity of Wittgenstein's Thought (Cornell, 1996) and Poetry at One Remove (Michigan, 1999).